Dragons

by Grace Hansen

Abdo Kids
WORLD OF MYTHICAL BEINGS

Abdo Kids Jumbo is an Imprint of Abdo Kids
abdobooks.com

abdobooks.com

Published by Abdo Kids, a division of ABDO, P.O. Box 398166, Minneapolis, Minnesota 55439.

Printed in the United States of America, North Mankato, Minnesota.

052022

092022

Photo Credits: Alamy, Getty Images, Granger Collection, Shutterstock

Production Contributors: Teddy Borth, Jennie Forsberg, Grace Hansen
Design Contributors: Candice Keimig, Pakou Moua

Library of Congress Control Number: 2021950557

Publisher's Cataloging-in-Publication Data

Names: Hansen, Grace, author.

Title: Dragons / by Grace Hansen.

Description: Minneapolis, Minnesota : Abdo Kids, 2023 | Series: World of mythical beings | Includes online resources and index.

Identifiers: ISBN 9781098261887 (lib. bdg.) | ISBN 9781098262723 (ebook) | ISBN 9781098263140 (Read-to-Me ebook)

Subjects: LCSH: Dragons--Juvenile literature. | Mythical animals--Juvenile literature. | Folklore--Juvenile literature. | Legends--Juvenile literature.

Classification: DDC 398.24--dc23

Table of Contents

Myth of the Dragon 4

Western Dragons 8

Eastern Dragons 14

Dragons Today 20

Dragons of the World 22

Glossary 23

Index 24

Abdo Kids Code 24

Myth of the Dragon

People have told stories about dragons for thousands of years. No one is sure when or where the first stories came from.

5

Ancient peoples sometimes found giant **fossils**. It was hard to imagine real animals of that size. Some historians believe stories were created to explain the fossils. This is how dragon myths may have come to be.

Western Dragons

Dragons look and act differently in certain parts of the world. Western dragons mainly come from European **lore**. Legends tell of fire-breathing, winged monsters.

Europe
Asia
Africa
N
W
E
S

In the west, dragons can be deadly and evil. They often live in caves and guard treasures.

Western dragons are covered in scales. They have a barbed tail. They soar across the sky, snatching up animals and people.

Eastern Dragons

Eastern dragons are very different. Large, snake-like creatures are described in Chinese **folklore**. They have scales, but are often wingless.

Europe
Asia
China
Africa
N
W
E
S

In Eastern legends, most dragons are kind helpers. They are symbols of goodness. The dragons are often shown holding a pearl, which represents things like power and **wisdom**.

Eastern dragons are magical. They can change their size or the way they look. These dragons often have control over nature. They can create clouds and rain or change the seasons.

Dragons Today

Today, dragons are found in books, movies, and on TV. They range from lovable sidekicks to very scary **foes**. Dragons are also still celebrated in many cultures.

Dragons of the World

Apep
Egypt

- An ancient Egyptian god
- A large, snake-like creature
- Wanted to eat the sun
- Embodied chaos

Asian Lung
China

- Flies without wings
- Long, whisker-like feelers and a mane
- Often found near water

Beowulf's Dragon
Great Britain

- Breathes fire
- Guards its treasure
- Covered in tough scales, except for its belly

Fafnir
Scandinavia

- Covered in scales
- Guards gold
- Eating its heart gives one knowledge
- Inspired the dragon Smaug in J.R.R. Tolkien's *The Hobbit*

Glossary

foe – an enemy.

folklore – the stories and ways of a group of people from a certain place or country.

fossil – the remains or trace of a living animal or plant from a long time ago.

lore – all the facts and traditions about a particular subject that have been collected over time.

wisdom – good judgment and an understanding of that which is true and good.

Index

characteristics 10, 16, 20

Chinese mythology 14, 16, 18

depictions 8, 10, 12, 14, 16

European mythology 8, 10, 12

fire breathing 8

fossils 6

human interaction 12, 16

magical ability 18

media 20

pearl 16

scales 12, 14

shapeshifting 18

size 6, 14, 18

wings 8, 14

Visit **abdokids.com**

to access crafts, games,

videos, and more!

Use Abdo Kids code

WDK1887

or scan this QR code!